MIRROR image

Workbook and Discussion Guide

12 SESSIONS FOR PERSONAL OR GROUP STUDY

SYLVIA FERRIN

MIRROR IMAGE
Workbook and Discussion Guide

Copyright © 2019 by Sylvia Ferrin

Printed in the United States of America.

ISBN 978-0-9800943-7-4

All rights reserved. No part of this book may be copied, modified and/or reproduced by electronic, mechanical or other means, without written permission of the author.

All Scripture references are from the KJV of the Bible.

Author Photograph by 630 Design and Photography

Cover design by Chase Stamp

To order additional copies, visit:
www.magnifytheword.com
www.mkt.com/FerrinBookstore

This Mirror Image
Workbook and Discussion Guide
belongs to:

_____

CONTENTS

Introduction 7
Suggested Study Plans 9
Session Segments 11
15 Tips for Group Leaders 13

1. Defining Beauty/God's Ideal Woman 17

2. Female Competition/God's Beauty Pageant 23

3. Media Madness/Live Life 29

4. Divine Design/Better with Age 35

5. Modesty Matters/Modesty Still Matters 41

6. Objections to Modesty/Ambassadors 47

7. Made Up/Gender Values 53

8. Clothing/Hair 59

9. Women of Valor/Winning the War 65

10. Three Basic Beauty Tips/A Beautiful Attitude .. 71

11. Shopping with God/Godly Garments 77

12. See and Be Seen/Beautiful in God's Sight 83

Answer Key 89
Notes 95

INTRODUCTION

Welcome to the Mirror Image Bible Study. You are about to embark on a wonderful journey.

Mirror Image – Workbook and Discussion Guide, which has 12 sessions, is a companion to *Mirror Image – Beautiful in God's Sight,* which has 24 chapters. Each session in the *Mirror Image – Workbook and Discussion Guide* corresponds to two chapters in *Mirror Image – Beautiful in God's Sight.*

The Mirror Image Bible Study is designed to help girls and ladies break free from the pressure to conform to America's unrealistic beauty ideal. They will be encouraged to accept and embrace their natural beauty.

This 12-session study is ideal for a number of teaching environments, including small group study, book clubs, Bible studies, Sunday School classes, ladies meetings, and personal study.

Each session combines six segments for an effective and enjoyable Bible study: Key Verse, Study Questions, Looking in the Mirror, Discussion Points, Prayer Time, and Personal Reflections.

SUGGESTED STUDY PLANS

THE ONE-YEAR PLAN
Many churches schedule ladies meetings that meet once a month. Because *Mirror Image* has 12 sessions that correspond to the 12 months of the year, it is an ideal curriculum for monthly ladies meetings.

THE THREE-MONTH PLAN
The Three-Month Plan is ideal for Bible study groups or Sunday School classes that meet weekly. Using *Mirror Image* as your curriculum, you can work through the 12 sessions within a quarter, or a three-month period.

THE SELF-STUDY PLAN
If you want to use *Mirror Image* as a personal study curriculum, you can proceed according to your own timetable. I do, however, suggest that you maintain some sort of schedule to keep from getting sidetracked for extended periods of time.

SESSION SEGMENTS

Each session chapter contains six basic segments, designed to guide you through each lesson.

KEY VERSE

Each session has a key verse that sets the theme for that topic. It is located on the first page of each session chapter. You may want to commit this verse to memory.

STUDY QUESTIONS

Each session has fill-in-the-blank questions. Answers to these questions are *italicized* and easily found within the corresponding chapters in *Mirror Image – Beautiful in God's Sight*.

Before each session, take time to read the corresponding chapters of *Mirror Image – Beautiful in God's Sight*. As you read, watch for answers to the Study Questions.

LOOKING IN THE MIRROR

Within text boxes are brief thoughts designed to lead into Discussion Points. It might be helpful to have a participant read these thoughts aloud.

DISCUSSION POINTS

Discussion points are designed to promote openness in a safe and friendly environment. The questions are specifically crafted to stimulate discussion within an interactive group.

PRAYER TIME

This will be one of the most important aspects of your study time. *Mirror Image* addresses sensitive topics. In order for us to best understand God's values and thoughts concerning our physical appearance and attitudes, we must talk to Him.

Biblical concepts often oppose our society's norms. It is not easy to travel upstream and go against the flow. In order to adopt the Bible's way of thinking and make it a part of our own lives, we must pray and ask God to help us think the way He thinks, rather than the way the world around us thinks. When we pray about these biblical concepts, God will help us make needed changes in our lives.

PERSONAL REFLECTIONS

Use the Personal Reflections space to record how each session specifically affects you. This is where you process what you have learned in a group setting. If you have received understanding from the Lord and His Word, write down your thoughts.

It is quite likely that God will give you insight that is not even addressed in *Mirror Image – Beautiful in God's Sight*. He wants to personalize your journey as you grow into the woman He called you to be.

15 TIPS FOR GROUP LEADERS

1. Book and Workbook
The Mirror Image Bible Study combines *Mirror Image – Beautiful in God's Sight* with the *Workbook and Discussion Guide*. Participants should bring Bibles and both *Mirror Image* books to sessions.

2. Planning and Note Taking
While planning for each session, use *Mirror Image – Beautiful in God's Sight* as a springboard. Highlight key points that you find particularly insightful, make notes in the margin of the book and jot down relevant Scriptures that come to your mind. This will help you as you lead discussions.

3. Six Segments
Each session is divided into six segments: Key Verse, Study Questions, Looking in the Mirror, Discussion Points, Prayer Time, and Personal Reflections. Guide participants through each segment of this teaching format.

4. Pre-Session Reading
Ask participants to read the corresponding chapters in *Mirror Image – Beautiful in God's Sight* prior to each session. Reading the book will optimize spiritual growth as a result of this study.

5. Memorize Key Verses
You may want to use the Key Verse (located on the first page of each chapter) as a memory verse.

6. Pre-Session Study Questions

Ask participants to fill in the Study Questions prior to each session. Review these during sessions.

7. Discussion Points

Open discussion is an effective way to learn so be sure to allot sufficient time in each session for participants to share their thoughts and experiences.

The topics in *Mirror Image* could potentially generate a lot of discussion. That is good. You want participants to talk and share their ideas and experiences.

But if the discussions become too opinionated, argumentative or heated, steer the ladies back to the study and assure them that the answers they seek are all found in the Bible. Keep them focused on the study.

As you facilitate interactive conversation, encourage everyone to participate. However, if some people do not join in, they will still glean from what others have to share.

Again, as much as possible, keep discussions focused on the topic at hand. It is easy for conversations to get off target. Gently but kindly steer people back to the main subject.

8. Be Open and Transparent

You probably have stories of your own about how God helped you as you grew in your walk with Him and accepted your natural beauty instead of relying on externals to affirm you.

Be sure to share these experiences. Your openness will encourage others. As the group leader, participants will benefit from knowing that you overcame the things they currently struggle with.

9. Conclude with Prayer

Conclude each session with prayer. Pray specifically that God will help the participants to apply to their lives what they learned in the session.

10. Answer Key

The Answer Key for the Study Questions is in the back of the workbook. Encourage participants to not look at the Answer Key unless they have difficulty locating the answers as they read *Mirror Image – Beautiful in God's Sight*.

11. Create a Welcoming Environment

The Mirror Image Bible Study is designed for settings that are conducive to open discussion and fellowship. I recommend a casual setting where ladies can gather in a living room or around a table or sit in chairs arranged in a circle.

A successful Bible study is one where an individual grows close not just to God, but also to the body of Christ. A more relaxed setting will encourage them to take down their guard.

Light snacks and beverages are optional but often help people feel more comfortable.

12. Make Guests Comfortable

Guests unfamiliar with our apostolic lifestyle will probably be able to grasp the logic in the material presented. But it may surprise some guests that certain concepts are biblical. Do not presume that they have knowledge that you might take for granted or that they understand everything you teach. Be sensitive and considerate and help them feel as comfortable as possible.

13. Attendance

This may sound too formal, but you might want to assign someone to keep attendance records.

When someone misses a session, contact them and let them know they were missed.

14. 90 Minutes

From start to finish, I recommend that each session be no longer than 90 minutes. This is enough time to cover all segments of the *Workbook and Discussion Guide* without tiring the participants. Also, start on time. Don't wait for chronic stragglers.

15. Seek God's Guidance

Last but certainly not least, pray before each session for God to guide your thoughts and words and for His blessing to be upon each participant. Be compassionate and sensitive to people as they express their thoughts and experiences. Expect God to do great things in each life as you study His Word!

SESSION 1

Defining Beauty
God's Ideal Woman

Favour is deceitful,
and beauty is vain:
but a woman that feareth the LORD,
she shall be praised.

Proverbs 31:30

MIRROR IMAGE

STUDY QUESTIONS

1. Each society on the globe has an ideal of _____ that differs from other societies.

2. Most, if not all, societies define beauty _____ of how most women of that nationality naturally look.

3. The moment a woman is born into the framework of her society, she instinctively adopts its ideals without _____.

4. At a time when girls should be enjoying their _____ and growing into womanhood, they are often obsessed with and even distressed by their _____.

5. Our society places a high priority on flawlessness. It exalts its flawed ideal of beauty as something very few women naturally have: _____.

6. Throughout an American woman's lifetime, she will have experienced the _____ to conform to several different ideologies of beauty.

7. Unlike American society's out-of-reach, unattainable, unrealistic beauty standard, God's beauty ideal is accessible to _____ woman, everywhere.

8. God's ideal of beauty is far _____ from society's ideal of beauty.

9. As we adopt a biblical perspective to the beauty dilemma, we will find ourselves _____.

10. Rather than a movie star, model, or celebrity, the Proverbs ____ woman can be our ideal.

LOOKING IN THE MIRROR

Some people see Christianity as demanding and restrictive. But considering the promises and benefits available to those who follow Jesus, Christianity is actually a life of hope, joy, peace, and contentment. Sounds like liberty to me!

What *is* demanding and restrictive is the world's system. One of their tactics is to define beauty with an unrealistic standard and then promise women fulfillment if they adopt their ideal.

Women who comply with this human-based system do not find fulfillment. But when our view of beauty is God-based, we are liberated from the shifting ideas of our culture. We are free to look in our mirrors and see past the external, receiving God's promises and enjoying His benefits.

MIRROR IMAGE

DISCUSSION POINTS

1. How would you define America's ideal woman?

_____
_____
_____
_____
_____
_____

2. How does America's ideal woman differ from God's ideal woman?

_____
_____
_____
_____
_____
_____

3. Read "Ideal Woman Checklist" on pages 30-34. List one quality you have and one quality you can work on implementing into your life.

_____
_____
_____
_____
_____
_____

PRAYER TIME

Jesus, even from the time I was a little girl, my mind has been shaped by my culture's definition of beauty, which is vastly different from yours. My society's standard of beauty is so unfulfilling. It is not a God-centered standard, but one based upon the ever-shifting whims of the fashion and entertainment industries.

I am so glad that your beauty ideal is attainable to every woman, everywhere. I am so glad that your plan for my life does not include me living with feelings of inadequacy about my physical appearance. I am thankful that when I adopt your value system, you extend grace to me as I grow into the woman you designed me to be.

God, please help me to resist the pressure to conform to my society's ever-changing beauty ideal. I want to define beauty according to your definition. Instead of looking to the world for my ideal of beauty, help me to look into your Word.

Thank you for liberating me from the expectations and beauty standards of people who do not know you. Thank you for giving me an alternative beauty standard, one which focuses on women in your Word who serve as godly, virtuous role models.

MIRROR IMAGE

PERSONAL REFLECTIONS

SESSION 2

Female Competition
God's Beauty Pageant

Many daughters have done virtuously,
but thou excellest them all.

Proverbs 31:29

MIRROR IMAGE

STUDY QUESTIONS

1. Body dissatisfaction early on in life is due in large part to the _____ young ladies make between themselves and others.

2. Most _____ cannot relate to the body dissatisfaction that plagues many women.

3. Because of our tendency to ruthlessly criticize ourselves and _____ ourselves with other women, we are easy prey to advertising predators.

4. Women who are secure in Jesus do not need to _____ themselves by tearing others down.

5. Constantly worrying about what other people think of us produces self-imposed _____.

6. We can _____ win God's Beauty Pageant!

7. There is constant pressure on Bible believers to adopt the world's _____.

8. What people can see is not the sum _____ of who we are.

9. Get your _____ from your _____ in Christ.

10. Your relationship with _____ is the most important relationship in your life.

> ## LOOKING IN THE MIRROR
>
> Our society has many competitive activities. For example, sports is big business, fueled by fans' desire to be associated with a winning team.
>
> To an extent, our education system is competitive. Ambitious young people strive to rise to the top of their class, then attempt to be accepted to top universities in order to get top paying jobs. This all requires them to be competitive and get an edge on other people.
>
> We all want to be winners. Who plays a game with the goal of losing? Nobody. But when it comes to females competing with each other in a subtle but catty way, the result is anything but beautiful.
>
> Instead of having a competitive attitude, maybe we should compliment one another...sincerely. Rather than envy another woman, it is okay to acknowledge her strengths without either demeaning or exalting ourselves.
>
> Life's too short to waste time comparing ourselves to other women. After all, in God's beauty pageant, we are *all* winners!

MIRROR IMAGE

DISCUSSION POINTS

1. Have you ever mentally compared your talents, appearance, achievements, social status, or family prominence to another woman?
Circle One: YES or NO

2. Do you fret about what people think about you to the point where you cannot relax and be yourself?
Circle One: YES or NO

3. Do you yearn for the approval of people and feel let down and disappointed when you do not get it?
Circle One: YES or NO

4. Read the bullet points in "What God Values" on pages 48-51. Which one identifies a worldly value that you need to replace with God's value?

_____
_____
_____
_____

5. List the Fabulous Five ways to display true beauty.

_____
_____
_____
_____

PRAYER TIME

Jesus, females can be unkind when we get around each other. What is it that motivates us to compare ourselves to each other? It seems we have this built-in detection system to gauge ourselves by other women.

I don't like the unpleasant feeling I get when I compare myself to other women. Jesus, please help me to shed this competitive spirit once and for all. Help me to find my contentment in you, not in my physical appearance, achievements, or status.

The only competition I want to be in is your beauty pageant. In your beauty pageant, *all* godly ladies are winners. We don't compete against one another, but strive to please you and you alone. As we each adopt your values, we find ourselves beautified by your Word and your Spirit.

I want to value the things you value and disesteem any worldly values that oppose your Kingdom. I want to win your beauty pageant! I want to be beautiful in your sight.

MIRROR IMAGE

PERSONAL REFLECTIONS

_____
_____
_____
_____
_____
_____
_____
_____
_____
_____
_____
_____
_____
_____
_____
_____
_____
_____
_____
_____
_____
_____
_____
_____

SESSION 3

Media Madness
Live Life

Finally, brethren, whatsoever things are true, whatsoever things are honest, whatsoever things are just, whatsoever things are pure, whatsoever things are lovely, whatsoever things are of good report; if there be any virtue, and if there be any praise, think on these things.

Philippians 4:8

MIRROR IMAGE

STUDY QUESTIONS

1. America's ideal of beauty stems from and is almost exclusively propagated by _____.

2. When regular women _____ their bodies to Hollywood stars, most fall short.

3. Using artificial means, producers create _____ which are an _____ rather than _____.

4. The entertainment industry is designed to influence us as it creates for us their concept of what is _____.

5. When American women compare themselves to Hollywood, they allow their own _____ to be trumped by image and _____.

6. Hollywood is a _____.

7. If you look at Hollywood, which many Americans allow to set the standard of beauty for them, you will see the exact _____ of _____ standard of beauty.

8. In more ways than one, Hollywood has a perverted definition of _____ and _____.

9. Mainstream movies are not made in the _____ of _____. They are _____ images designed to lure people away from God.

10. Only after you destroy media's grip on your life will you realize how it has been holding you _____ to its _____.

LOOKING IN THE MIRROR

Americans spend over 10 hours a day consuming media in various forms. Wow. That is a lot of time!

Afraid of not being "in the know" about a new popular show, the latest celebrity scandal, or what your friend ate for breakfast? Relax. Your life is much more grand than anything movies, live streaming, YouTube, or social media can offer.

Honestly examine your media viewing habits:
- How much of it is contributing positively to your life?
- Is creating and maintaining an online persona more important than real communication with people who truly love you?
- What can you cut out so you can make time for more meaningful and productive activities?

MIRROR IMAGE

DISCUSSION POINTS

1. Have you ever been fascinated and enthralled by a celebrity, movie star, or other entertainer?
Circle One: YES or NO

2. Do you think that the content of Hollywood movies has more of a *positive* or *negative* effect on the body image of girls and women?

_____

3. Have you ever had negative thoughts about yourself during or after viewing media which portrayed movie stars and models as "perfect"?
Circle One: YES or NO

4. List three activities from the "Live Life List" that interest you which you can use to replace the time you spend viewing media.

_____
_____
_____
_____
_____
_____
_____
_____
_____

PRAYER TIME

Jesus, media is such an influential part of my society. Everywhere I turn it seems like the world, in the form of visual entertainment, is vying for my heart.

Not only is media time consuming, but it can also eat away at my pure love for you, slowly eroding my desire for spiritual things. Sometimes, I just want to relax and be entertained but afterwards, I feel empty.

So much of media opposes your holy Word. I don't want anything to take your place on the throne of my heart. Help me to replace the time I spend watching worldly movies with more productive activities. I know you have a purpose for my life and I don't want to squander it on things that are meaningless. Even social media has the potential to be distracting and bring me down to a level lower than you have designed for me to live. I don't want *anything* to rob me of my relationship with you.

Create in me a deeper sensitivity to you so that I can hear your voice rather than the voices of movie stars, the majority of which vehemently oppose you and your precious Word. Let your voice be what influences my life.

Thank you, Jesus, for liberating me from media madness and giving me a life worth living!

MIRROR IMAGE

PERSONAL REFLECTIONS

SESSION 4

Divine Design
Better with Age

I will praise thee;
for I am fearfully and wonderfully made:
marvellous are thy works;
and that my soul knoweth right well.

Psalm 139:14

MIRROR IMAGE

STUDY QUESTIONS

1. God does _____ think you are ugly.

2. Pretending to be someone or something we are not is a hard _____ to maintain.

3. We can all portray our personal style through our clothes and still look _____, _____, and _____ in a godly way.

4. God values _____, but He also esteems _____ _____.

5. No matter how old we are, we should never stop _____, learning, and sharpening our _____ so it will become more and more like the Lord's.

6. Each stage of life is beautiful. There is _____ in youth and _____ in old age and every stage in between.

7. As we age, we should become _____, not _____. Our walks with God should grow _____, not _____.

8. The world has their methods of achieving _____ beauty. God has His methods that allow us to achieve _____ beauty.

9. Instead of resenting _____, we should be thankful we have lived long enough to get them!

10. Dyeing your hair is like a lie you have to keep telling. Once you dye your hair an _____ color, you have to continually maintain the facade you have created.

LOOKING IN THE MIRROR

Take a look at nature and you will get the idea that God likes variety. Studies show that our Earth has over 10,000 species of birds, over 60,000 species of trees, and over 400,000 species of flowering plants. Sounds incredible, doesn't it? God could have created nature to be mundane and monochrome but He didn't. Nature is God's canvas and He fashioned a brilliant masterpiece.

The same is true with human beings. We come in a variety of sizes and shapes. Our artisan Creator crafted us with a range of hair, skin, and eye colors. He designed us each to be unique.

As we age, our appearance changes but we are still unique. Just as God knew what He was doing when He created each type of bird, tree, and flowering plant, He knew what He was doing when He created us!

MIRROR IMAGE

DISCUSSION POINTS

1. When you look in the mirror, do you ever think negative thoughts about yourself?
Circle One: YES or NO

2. Do you ever wish you looked like another woman? When you view mass media, social media, or women's magazines, do you ever feel less than? Have you ever envied a woman that you think is beautiful who seems to have it all together? If you answered yes to any of these questions, write and say aloud Psalm 139:14.

_____
_____
_____
_____
_____

3. How old are you? _____

4. Which sign of aging bothers you the most?
_____
_____

5. What is a positive, productive activity that you can engage in during the current season of your life?
_____
_____
_____

PRAYER TIME

Jesus, when I look in the mirror, I sometimes focus on my flaws and imperfections. At times, I even mentally berate myself for how I look.

I know that I am not "perfect" according to my society's concept of an ideal woman. But you created me and designed me with my height, hair color, eye color, and facial features. You do not think I am ugly! You love me with an everlasting love.

Instead of wasting my time wishing I looked differently than I do, help me to humbly accept myself the way you made me. Help me to stop comparing myself to anyone else.

Also, help me to enjoy every season of my life. From my youth to my old age, I want to praise you! I want every season to bring you glory. I don't want to waste precious time wishing I was younger than I am, but I want to enjoy this life you have given me.

Thank you, Jesus, for creating me! I truly am "fearfully and wonderfully made." Help me to walk before you in humble awareness of your love for me.

MIRROR IMAGE

PERSONAL REFLECTIONS

SESSION 5

Modesty Matters
Modesty Still Matters

In like manner also, that women adorn themselves in modest apparel, with shamefacedness and sobriety; not with broided hair, or gold, or pearls, or costly array; But (which becometh women professing godliness) with good works.

I Timothy 2:9-10

MIRROR IMAGE

STUDY QUESTIONS

1. Our _____ has _____ immodesty.

2. _____ created modesty.

3. The subject of modesty _____ women.

4. Modesty is an _____ of inner virtue and _____ to God.

5. Modesty matters to _____.

6. Immodesty creates _____. It distracts from God's design for women.

7. The world views _____ as a liability. God views meekness as an indispensable commodity, something of _____ _____, because we are relying on His strength, rather than our own.

8. When we dress immodestly, we reveal that we have bought into the lie that our bodies should be on display for _____ to see.

9. Modesty should be demonstrated, not only by our _____ appearance, but by our _____ character.

10. Our attitudes and garments should bring attention and _____ to God. Our behavior, words, demeanor, and clothing should all _____ Him.

LOOKING IN THE MIRROR

Reflecting a fashion industry trend, several designers are creating modest garments. Hemlines are lower and necklines are higher. "Covering up" is now the mantra of the fashion world. Citing "female empowerment" as the reason for more modest clothing choices, this brand of feminism says that modesty places power in the hands of the wearer, not the viewer. In other words, by dressing modestly, they send a message that a woman's identity is about more than her shape and curves.

It is nice that fashion is more modest right now. It gives us more options when we go shopping. But what will we do when the fashion industry reverts to risqué and revealing clothing?

The answer is easy. Regardless of the fashion world's shifting trends, we will continue to embrace modesty. The world of fashion will change, but God's Word remains the same.

MIRROR IMAGE

DISCUSSION POINTS

1. Explain how women use hair, jewelry, and clothing to adorn (beautify and decorate) themselves the wrong way. (See pages 142-144.)

_____
_____
_____
_____
_____

2. What are the five correct adornment methods listed by Peter and Paul? (See pages 144-150.)
#1 _____
#2 _____
#3 _____
#4 _____
#5 _____

3. Think about your modesty journey. Was there a time when you were not modest? Has God personally addressed specific modesty issues in your life? Write your experiences.

_____
_____
_____
_____
_____
_____

PRAYER TIME

Jesus, thank you for helping me realize that there is a right and a wrong way for me to beautify myself. I want to beautify myself with *your* methods. I understand that what you most value cannot be seen with human eyes.

I want to be a woman who is meek because, to you, this characteristic is "of great price." Thank you for helping me realize that meekness is not weakness, but it is actually a fruit of your Spirit that takes great strength to cultivate. I want to be a woman of "good works," so that others may see you in me. I want to not only dress modestly, but also have godly inner character that displays your attributes.

God, you are so wonderful! Thank you for helping me realize that you do not measure my worth by the world's measurements. Your gauge is not confined to my appearance, but you see me as a whole person. I am your child and I am so grateful to know that you love me with an everlasting love.

I want to honor you in my decisions about what I wear. Help me to make choices that draw attention to you, rather than my body. My body is the "temple" that you live in. When people see me, I want them to see you!

MIRROR IMAGE

PERSONAL REFLECTIONS

_____
_____
_____
_____
_____
_____
_____
_____
_____
_____
_____
_____
_____
_____
_____
_____
_____
_____
_____
_____

SESSION 6

Objections to Modesty Ambassadors

Now then we are ambassadors for Christ,
as though God did beseech you by us:
we pray you in Christ's stead,
be ye reconciled to God.

II Corinthians 5:20

MIRROR IMAGE

STUDY QUESTIONS

1. We don't cover our bodies because we consider them dirty or shameful, but because we have something worth _____.

2. According to the Bible, it is immodesty that is _____, not modesty.

3. Immodesty _____ pure God-designed sexuality and conveys that a woman is worth little more than her _____.

4. When a woman dresses immodestly, it draws attention to her _____. When she dresses modestly, it draws attention to her _____.

5. The accusation that a person who dresses modestly is in bondage is _____. The real definition of bondage is a woman who has to rely on external sources to feel acceptable and _____.

6. Modesty is _____ from a depraved society's devaluation of the human body.

7. Modesty is _____ bondage. Modesty is liberation.

8. God has sent us into this world to be His _____ representatives. We are His witnesses. We are His _____.

Objections to Modesty/Ambassadors

9. When we understand the beauty of our identity as daughters of the King, we don't want to wear a _____. We don't want to be undercover Christians and _____ in.

10. Keep your _____ intact...inside and outside.

LOOKING IN THE MIRROR

When we talk about modesty, some people may conclude that we have a condescending "us and them" mentality. This is not true. I don't believe that most apostolic ladies consider themselves superior to other people.

But our relationship to the King of kings does make us different. When we are born again of the water and the Spirit, we enter the Kingdom of God. When we are Jesus' disciples, we are "not of this world" but are sent "into the world" (John 17:14-18).

We are not to partake of the mindsets and attitudes "of this world" but we are to be Jesus' ambassadors "into the world."

Inside and outside, we can portray to the world the message God wants them to hear.

MIRROR IMAGE

DISCUSSION POINTS

1. Do you think *modesty* or *immodesty* gives women more reliable security? _____

2. Has anyone ever made fun of you or accused you of being "bound" or legalistic because of your modest appearance?
Circle One: YES or NO

3. Has anyone ever shown you respect because of your modest appearance?
Circle One: YES or NO

2. Describe how modesty protects women.
_____
_____
_____
_____
_____
_____

3. Has there ever been a time when your modest appearance prompted questions from people, allowing you to share Jesus with them? If so, describe your experience.
_____
_____
_____
_____
_____

PRAYER TIME

God, my culture gives many arguments against modesty. They think it is shameful and old-fashioned. I cover my body, not because I am ashamed of it, but because I have something worth protecting. My body, which is your temple, is valuable and you do not want it to be displayed to just anyone.

I do not view modesty as prohibitive or restrictive. Rather, modesty is liberation from society's corrupt glorification of the human body.

Regardless of what *people* think, I want to always remember that *you* created modesty. To you, immodesty is shameful but modesty is honorable.

I am your visual representative to a world that is so lost, hurting and sad. If I blend and adopt their clothing, attitudes, thoughts, and speech, I will squelch your light within me. If I am just like them, then I will have no hope to offer them.

Help me to – inside and outside – accurately portray the values of your Kingdom. I am your ambassador and I want to represent you and do your work on this earth in a way that pleases you.

MIRROR IMAGE

PERSONAL REFLECTIONS

_____
_____
_____
_____
_____
_____
_____
_____
_____
_____
_____
_____
_____
_____
_____
_____
_____
_____
_____
_____
_____
_____

SESSION 7

Made Up Gender Values

They looked unto him, and were lightened:
and their faces were not ashamed.
Psalm 34:5

...male and female created he them.
Genesis 1:27

MIRROR IMAGE

STUDY QUESTIONS

1. It was not God's plan for Eve, the mother of all living, and God's first created woman, to feel inadequate and _____ without the application of _____ to her face. She was _____ just the way she was.

2. God never intended for us to gain our confidence from ourselves, our appearance, or from how other people perceive us. He alone wants to be the source of our _____!

3. God wants us to know and believe that He _____ us regardless of our imperfections.

4. Your _____ is a beautiful ornament that money _____ buy.

5. Rather than encouraging men and women to work together in _____, feminists promote gender _____.

6. A truly feminine _____ displays kindness, sensitivity, and gentle beauty.

7. Role _____ does not work. It creates _____.

8. God chose for each gender's unique role and biological differences to be displayed by our choice of _____ and _____ length.

9. When it comes to our behavior, physical appearance, mindset, and attitude, we need to look into the mirror of the _____ of God, not the mirror of the _____.

10. There is a clear _____ between the breakdown in America of biblical gender _____, women wearing _____, and women cutting their _____.

LOOKING IN THE MIRROR

No apologies necessary! If you are a woman, be glad. If you are a man, be glad. Our society is normalizing body modifications so that a man can look like a woman, and vice versa.

The unique nature of each gender is not something to despise, but something to appreciate. It is okay to reflect your gender identity through your mindset, behavior, speech, and appearance. Celebrate who you are as a precious creation of your loving Father.

MIRROR IMAGE

DISCUSSION POINTS

1. List The Super Seven biblical and common sense principles about makeup. (See pages 202-211.)
#1 _____
#2 _____
#3 _____
#4 _____
#5 _____
#6 _____
#7 _____

2. Read "Unfeminine Feminism" (pages 220-223). How has the feminist movement distorted God's design for men and women's unique gender roles?
_____
_____
_____
_____
_____

3. What is an "alpha female?" (See pages 225-227.)
_____
_____
_____
_____
_____

4. Do outward gender distinctives prevent confusion and help maintain order in families and society? Choose One: YES or NO

PRAYER TIME

Jesus, thank you for my face. It enables me to express your love to the world. My eyes can show forth your kindness and compassion. My ears can listen to people as they share their hurts. My mouth can smile, brightening lives, and speak words of love and truth.

When I look in the mirror, help me to know that, just as you created my arms, legs, hands, and feet, you also created my face. Just because my face has a few "flaws" does not mean that I need to cover them up. You love me as I am. I do not look down on women who wear makeup, but I know that you never told me to wear makeup and I am glad that I am not any less acceptable to you without it.

You designed me to be a woman. In a culture that continues to aggressively redefine what it means for a man to be a man and a woman to be a woman, it takes courage to form Bible-based gender values.

Being a woman does not mean that I am inferior to men; it simply means I am different from them. And that is more than okay. You designed us to be different.

We display our gender differences outwardly to prevent confusion and promote harmony. God, your ways are always right!

MIRROR IMAGE

PERSONAL REFLECTIONS

_____
_____
_____
_____
_____
_____
_____
_____
_____
_____
_____
_____
_____
_____
_____
_____
_____
_____
_____
_____
_____
_____
_____
_____
_____

SESSION 8

Clothing
Hair

The woman shall not wear
that which pertaineth unto a man...
Deuteronomy 22:5

But if a woman have long hair, it is a glory to her:
for her hair is given her for a covering.
I Corinthians 11:15

MIRROR IMAGE

STUDY QUESTIONS

1. God wants _____ and _____ to maintain distinctiveness in their genders, their roles and their clothing.

2. When women assumed the _____ of men, they also put on their _____.

3. Women wearing pants was more than mere rebellion against what women considered outdated clothing. It was rebellion against an entire system based upon _____.

4. Social acceptance is _____ a good basis upon which to form our _____.

5. Pants are a distinctively _____ garment that designers _____ to fit women's bodies.

6. _____ hair on women and _____ hair on men is a _____ gender distinctive that is specifically mentioned in the Bible.

7. In America, just as women did not wear _____ until the _____ movement gained momentum, so women in America did not _____ their _____.

8. God has equipped women with a _____, built-in covering: Her _____.

Clothing/Hair

9. In the Bible, hair is _____.
_____ hair on a woman and _____ hair on a man symbolize submission to God's gender values.

10. It is an _____ to show forth in our _____ and _____ our unique God-given _____ _____.

LOOKING IN THE MIRROR

Have you ever seen a person and been unsure if you were looking at a man or a woman? When we do things God's way, people never have to look at us and wonder which gender we are.

One of the ways a Christian lady displays that she accepts her God-given gender is through her hair and clothing. Despite feminists' efforts, there are still women who don't want to look less feminine. They enjoy who they are as gracious, godly ladies.

Thank God for your built-in covering of hair and the opportunity to dress like a lady. Be comfortable with your gender identity. Not only will your contentment with your feminine appearance benefit you, but as other women observe you, they might be encouraged to also adopt a more feminine mindset and lifestyle.

MIRROR IMAGE

DISCUSSION POINTS

1. List the three steps of social change. (See "Normalizing the Abnormal" on page 242.)
#1 _____
#2 _____
#3 _____

2. Based on what you have learned by reading "Chapter 15 – Clothing: A Gender Distinctive," describe how modest skirts and dresses are an expression of biblical femininity.

_____
_____
_____
_____
_____

3. What are the themes of I Corinthians 11:3-16? (See page 252.)
#1 _____
#2 _____
#3 _____
#4 _____

4. According to I Corinthians 11:15, what is a woman's covering? _____

5. Is short hair on men and long hair on women symbolic of compliance with God's gender values? Circle One: YES or NO

PRAYER TIME

Lord, two of the most significant ways I can display my female gender identity is by my clothing and my hair. Thank you for all I have learned about how feminists in America have succeeded at breaking down these visible signs of gender distinction. Their anti-God agenda opposes your Word and I do not want to be affiliated with it in any way. Certainly, you highly value women, but the way feminists go about trying to prove themselves completely opposes your plan.

Thank you for the opportunity to dress like a woman in modest skirts and dresses and for the built-in covering of hair you have given me. You designed men and women to be different and we can portray those differences through our outward appearance.

Yes, I know that many people consider it outdated for women to wear skirts exclusively and wear their hair long. But your ways never change. You have always wanted a demarcation between genders.

Thank you, Lord, for giving me understanding about how to display my unique gender identity through my clothing and hair. You are truly wonderful, wise and perfect in all your ways.

MIRROR IMAGE

PERSONAL REFLECTIONS

SESSION 9

Women of Valor
Winning the War

Who can find a virtuous woman?
for her price is far above rubies.

Proverbs 31:10

STUDY QUESTIONS

1. Submission's primary purpose is achieving and maintaining _____ in marriages, families, churches, countries, militaries, and workplaces.

2. Submission is not about your _____ being taken away. Rather, it helps protect and _____ your rights.

3. _____ did not create submission. _____ did.

4. A marriage will never work harmoniously if the _____ thinks she is independent from and _____ to her husband.

5. If we wait for our _____ to become _____ before we submit to them, we will never submit!

6. Submission is for _____, whether married or single, male or female.

7. In the Bible, submission is a voluntary action. It is a _____. God never forces anyone to submit.

8. You can gauge whether or not you are truly submitted, not only by your actions, but also by your _____ and your _____.

9. Allow your husband to be your _____.

10. We will never become truly submissive without making it a matter of _____.

LOOKING IN THE MIRROR

Let's face it. We are not born submitted. All of us – male and female – learn how to say "no" at a young age. We are born wanting things our own way. We don't want to answer to anybody.

Rethinking our approach to submission requires us to PRAY. We will never be truly submissive without prayer. We will not become submissive by simply exercising our willpower. Certainly, we must put forth effort to be submissive, but a truly submissive attitude is only ours when we pray and allow God to transform our minds.

When you struggle with submission, remember that your greatest example – Jesus Christ – was submissive. In the Garden of Gethsemane, He struggled too. He did not want to submit to the will of God. But He prayed until His will died.

That's what we have to do. When we pray and spend time in God's presence, what is repulsive to the world – submission – becomes beautiful to us. So pray and enjoy God's hand at work in your life.

MIRROR IMAGE

DISCUSSION POINTS

1. Complete this formula (page 268):
Order = _____
Disorder = _____

2. List three reasons (pages 275-276) why some women hate the mention of submission. Can you think of other reasons why women hate submission?
#1 _____
#2 _____
#3 _____
Other Reasons: _____
_____
_____
_____
_____

3. Was Jesus submissive to the Father's will?
Circle One: YES or NO

4. Write down some of the blessings and benefits of submission. _____
_____
_____
_____
_____
_____
_____

PRAYER TIME

Jesus, I live in a culture where submission is mocked and rebellion is glorified. My culture pressures me to rebel, to resist, to be independent.

But your precious Word tells me that submission is the path to peace. Submission does not come naturally to me and I desperately need you to change my heart. Help me to love your Word and help me to allow your Spirit to work in my life. I want to trade in my self-reliant mindset for a heart that is pliable and tender before you.

My leaders may not always do everything right but as long as they love you and are doing their best to please you, I know that you will bless me if I submit to them.

Help me to honor my husband, to love him and submit to him. As he continues to serve you, I know that you will guide him to make any necessary changes in his life without me nagging him or trying to take control of our relationship.

Submission to you, your Word, and your plan is counter-cultural. Even some of my closest friends and family resist submission. I do not want to follow in their footsteps in this area. I want to be a woman of valor…a truly virtuous woman!

MIRROR IMAGE

PERSONAL REFLECTIONS

SESSION 10

Three Basic Beauty Tips
A Beautiful Attitude

With all lowliness and meekness,
with longsuffering,
forbearing one another in love;
Endeavoring to keep the unity of the Spirit
in the bond of peace.

Ephesians 4:2-3

MIRROR IMAGE

STUDY QUESTIONS

1. A _____ person is known to be a person of understanding, perception, and _____ judgment.

2. A _____ woman is a beautiful woman…a truly _____ woman.

3. The Bible is filled with _____ that are powerful enough to transcend time and be applicable to _____ generation, _____ era, _____ society, and _____ culture.

4. As we seek to please God with our lives, we shine forth with _____-_____ confidence.

5. How we look, what we do or don't do, and our biblical convictions, whether in Word or principle, should always be portrayed with a beautiful _____!

6. _____, _____ and longsuffering are beautiful.

7. It is possible to compromise neither our _____ nor our genuine _____ for people.

8. Our society's "Don't judge me" attitude tries to intimidate anyone who draws _____.

9. We cannot quit speaking _____ just because some people are super-sensitive and misconstrue our _____.

10. We will not always _____, but we should always _____.

LOOKING IN THE MIRROR

As we walk through life, if we do not keep in mind the importance of discretion, principles, and pleasing God, we can get distracted and derailed from our God-given purpose.

Not only can discretion, principles, and pleasing God keep us from making bad choices in our day-to-day lives, but they can also prevent us from harboring bad attitudes about others.

Our natural inclination is to be judgmental and to compare ourselves to others. But God wants us to live in His supernatural realm, where kindness, grace, and mercy are in abundant supply. Even when we try to help people improve their lives, we must make sure that our motives, words, demeanor, and approach are all pleasing to God.

MIRROR IMAGE

DISCUSSION POINTS

1. List "Three Basic Beauty Tips" (page 299).
#1 _____
#2 _____
#3 _____

2. What does the word "discretion" mean?
_____
_____
_____

3. Describe the difference between a "rule" and a "principle." _____
_____
_____
_____
_____

4. Do you want to please God with your choices?
Circle One: YES or NO

5. Is it possible to be committed to biblical values and also be kind and loving toward people who disagree with you?
Circle One: YES or NO

6. Who do you know that has walked away from God because of inner hurt? _____
Make a point to pray for this person and show kindness to him or her in any way you can.

PRAYER TIME

Jesus, as I develop into the virtuous woman you created me to be, I need discretion. This is an unfamiliar concept to many people, but a discreet person is a person of understanding, perception, and good judgment. Life can present me with all sorts of unexpected dilemmas. Discretion can help me navigate every issue and make the right choices.

I also need to be guided by your principles. As I read your Word and listen to your Word being taught and preached, your principles will be imparted to me. They will also help me make proper choices.

More than anything, God, I want to please you. I know that your love for me never changes and for that I am so grateful. I will not always do everything right, but I really, really want to behave, think, speak, and dress in a way that pleases you.

There will be people who will disagree with how I live my life. Jesus, help me to always, always, always show forth your love to others. Even if we disagree with one another, I want to always have a beautiful attitude.

Lord, I praise you! Living for you and enjoying my relationship with you is the best thing that has ever happened to me. You are truly awesome!

MIRROR IMAGE

PERSONAL REFLECTIONS

SESSION 11

Shopping with God
Godly Garments

I put on righteousness,
and it clothed me.

Job 29:14

MIRROR IMAGE

STUDY QUESTIONS

1. We can get so focused on improving and enhancing ourselves outwardly that our _____ _____ can be neglected.

2. God is more interested in us _____ good than He is in us just _____ good.

3. There is no substitute for _____ when we need a priority adjustment.

4. After spending time in the presence of God, we peek out from our prayer closet and the world looks different. We have _____. We have been _____. We are _____, _____, and _____.

5. Learning to _____ in Jesus indicates that our _____ in Him is growing.

6. God's righteousness _____ our lives.

7. Our _____ clothes should be modest and discreet representations of our _____ garments of righteousness and salvation. What we have on the _____ should show up on the _____.

Shopping with God/Godly Garments

8. In the same way that we would change our _____, we are to change our spiritual _____.

9. Our behavior should reflect that we are putting off the _____ man (the works of the flesh) and putting on the _____ man (the fruit of the Spirit).

10. _____ clothes us with Christ!

LOOKING IN THE MIRROR

Isn't it wonderful to know that God is not just concerned about our outward appearance but He also offers us beautiful inner garments? Being beautiful in His sight is not confined to how we look on the outside.

God's garments allow us to shine forth with His righteousness. His love, joy, and peace are designed to bring calm to our minds and lives.

This is not a fairy tale. As we, through prayer and reading the Word, consecrate ourselves to Him more and more, we learn to live according to our royal identity.

MIRROR IMAGE

DISCUSSION POINTS

1. Write II Corinthians 5:17. _____
   _____
   _____
   _____
   _____
   _____

2. Read through the bullet points on pages 342-344. Do you use any of these coverings? If so, list them.
   _____
   _____

Ask God to help you trust Him more. As your security in Him grows, you will find that you no longer need your own coverings.

3. List the Armor of God. (See Ephesians 6:10-17.)
   _____
   _____
   _____

4. What does I Peter 5:5 tell us to wear?
   _____

5. What does Colossians 3:12-14 tell us to wear?
   _____
   _____
   _____

PRAYER TIME

Lord, it is one thing to talk about clothes that I can see. It is another thing altogether to talk about clothes that are invisible. These clothes are spiritual garments. Just as I need tangible clothing to cover and protect me, I also need your spiritual garments.

I can't find these garments at the mall or at the secondhand store. I can't buy them online and have them shipped to my home. No, your clothes are only available in my prayer closet. I obtain these garments as I draw closer to you, give you more of my heart, and learn to walk according to your will.

As I do, you cover me with "the robe of righteousness." You give me peace, rest, and joy. No, I definitely cannot purchase these priceless treasures at the store. How about faith, purity, and love? Sounds like an amazing wardrobe any woman would want. And, Lord, I am no exception. I want every beautiful garment you want to give me.

Your Word tells me to put on mercy, kindness, humility, and meekness. These and other godly traits do not come naturally to me and must be developed but being able to wear your royal apparel is well worth the effort. Thank you, Lord, for such a wonderful supply of beautiful, always-in-style spiritual garments!

MIRROR IMAGE

PERSONAL REFLECTIONS

SESSION 12

See and Be Seen
Beautiful in God's Sight

One thing have I desired of the LORD,
that will I seek after; that I may dwell in the
house of the LORD all the days of my life,
to behold the beauty of the LORD,
and to enquire in his temple.

Psalm 27:4

MIRROR IMAGE

STUDY QUESTIONS

1. Understanding what it means to "see and be seen" God's way is the beauty _____ you have been looking for.

2. If you want to be beautiful, you must _____ at God and allow His presence to surround you.

3. God is beautiful! In fact, He is the originator of beauty. When we look at God, we behold _____ beauty.

4. The debilitating _____ that tells me I am not good enough, not pretty enough, and not acceptable enough dissipates in the presence of God.

5. The secret to _____ _____ is beholding the beauty of the Lord and living in His presence.

6. When we better understand how much God _____ us and how beautiful He thinks we are, it brings us up to a level of _____ that is impossible to realize from any other relationship.

7. The most beautiful asset you have is _____ shining through you.

8. God's beauty is not seen by spending hours in front of our own _____ but by spending hours gazing into the Word of God.

9. When we look into the Mirror of the Word, we want the image looking back at us to reflect _____ character rather than our _____.

10. When we _____ the mirror of the world, we no longer gauge ourselves according to the world's ideal, but we look to Christ and Christ alone as our _____ of perfect beauty.

LOOKING IN THE MIRROR

Go look in a mirror. Don't look away. For several moments, gaze at the image looking back at you.

Do you like what you see? Has your mirror image changed since you began this study? As you look in your mirror, are you content with the image looking back at you?

I hope you can, not boastfully or pridefully, but confidently and contentedly, say, "I am beautiful in God's sight!"

MIRROR IMAGE

DISCUSSION POINTS

1. Is "seeing" God and being seen by God the beauty secret many women search for?
Circle One: YES or NO

2. Describe what it feels like to be in the presence of God. _____
_____
_____
_____
_____
_____

3. Do you know a woman who "glows" with the glory of God? _____

4. Write II Corinthians 3:18. _____
_____
_____
_____
_____
_____

5. In order to be beautiful in God's sight, do we need to replace the mirror of the world with the mirror of the Word?
Circle One: YES or NO

PRAYER TIME

Jesus, as I near the end of this Bible study, I thank you for all you have shown me from your precious Word. I want to be the woman you designed me to be and display my femininity not only through graceful modesty, but I also want to have a beautiful attitude.

Lord, I long to know you better! You are the originator of beauty. When I behold you, I see perfect beauty. I cannot see you with my physical eyes, but oh, how I love to "see" you during times of prayer and worship. Even when I sing to you, I can feel your presence and I know you are near.

When I am in your presence, I feel complete. Safe. Content. Satisfied. God, only you can give me the assurance I crave.

When I am in your presence, I experience what it feels like to be considered beautiful by the One who matters most. Oh, God, I love you more than anyone or anything!

It is your light that illuminates my life. It is your Word that reminds me over and over again that I am your daughter. Since you are the King of kings, that makes me royalty! As I continue to be molded into your likeness, may my mirror image reflect you. I always want to be beautiful in your sight!

MIRROR IMAGE

PERSONAL REFLECTIONS

ANSWER KEY

Session 1 – Defining Beauty/God's Ideal Woman
1. beauty
2. opposite
3. question
4. youth, appearance
5. Perfection
6. pressure
7. every
8. different
9. liberated
10. 31

Session 2 – Female Competition/God's Beauty Pageant
1. comparisons
2. men
3. compare
4. exalt
5. anxiety
6. all
7. values
8. total
9. worth, identity
10. God

Session 3 – Media Madness/Live Life
1. Hollywood
2. compare
3. images, illusion, reality
4. normal
5. beauty, facade
6. portal
7. opposite, God's
8. right, wrong
9. image, God, phony
10. hostage, lies

Session 4 – Divine Design/Better with Age
1. not
2. act
3. tasteful, modest, stylish
4. youth, old age
5. growing, character
6. beauty, beauty
7. better, bitter, stronger, weaker
8. fleeting, lasting
9. wrinkles
10. unnatural

Session 5 – Modesty Matters/Modesty Still Matters
1. culture, normalized
2. God
3. polarizes
4. expression, devotion
5. God
6. confusion
7. meekness, great value
8. anyone
9. outward, inner
10. glory, honor

Session 6 – Objections to Modesty/Ambassadors
1. protecting
2. shameful
3. cheapens, body
4. body, face
5. erroneous, beautiful
6. freedom
7. not
8. visual, ambassadors
9. disguise, blend
10. identity

Session 7 – Made Up/Gender Values
1. ugly, makeup, complete
2. confidence
3. loves
4. smile, can't
5. harmony, competition
6. lady
7. reversal, confusion
8. clothing, hair
9. Word, world
10. connection, roles, pants, hair

Session 8 – Clothing/Hair
1. men, women
2. role, clothing
3. God
4. never, values
5. male, altered
6. Long, short, natural
7. pants, feminist, cut, hair
8. natural, hair
9. symbolic, Uncut, cut
10. honor, clothing, hair, gender identity

Session 9 – Women of Valor/Winning the War
1. order
2. rights, preserve
3. Men, God
4. wife, superior
5. leaders, perfect
6. everyone
7. choice
8. words, attitudes
9. hero
10. prayer

Session 10 – Three Basic Beauty Tips/A Beautiful Attitude
1. discreet, good
2. discreet, beautiful
3. principles, every, every, every, every
4. God-given
5. attitude
6. Love, kindness
7. values, love
8. lines
9. truth, motives
10. agree, love

Session 11 – Shopping with God/Godly Garments
1. inner character
2. being, looking
3. prayer
4. hope, renewed, refreshed, complete, calm
5. rest, confidence
6. clothes
7. physical, spiritual, inside, outside
8. clothes, character
9. old, new
10. Baptism

Session 12 – See and Be Seen/Beautiful in God's Sight
1. secret
2. look
3. perfect
4. lie
5. true beauty
6. loves, contentment
7. Jesus
8. mirrors
9. His, own
10. break, model

NOTES

NOTES